This is my land

This is my land

by MARTIN CAIDIN

photographs by
JAMES YARNELL

RANDOM HOUSE NEW YORK

Some other books by
MARTIN CAIDIN

GOLDEN WINGS
BLACK THURSDAY
THE LONG, LONELY LEAP
THUNDERBIRDS!
AIR FORCE
THE ASTRONAUTS
SPACEPORT U.S.A.

The photographs in this book were taken by a Honeywell Pentax camera.

Layout by MARTIN CAIDIN and FRED L. WOLFF

This book is for

OLIVE ANN BEECH

First light . . .

The first light of the sun to touch America each morning strikes
the peak of Mt. Katahdin in Maine, 5,267 feet above sea level.
Katahdin dominates the beautiful country around the town of Millinocket. The moment is exactly 4:45 A.M.; seconds later, soft light
spills down Katahdin's sides to bring dawn to lumber camps and
lodges along Lakes Nahmakanta, Molunkus, Brassua, Moosehead.

Lying beneath towering clouds, Key Largo is the southeasternmost corner
of America. From two miles above Rock Harbor, the water is a deep jade
color; the beaches form sharp white borderlines along the Florida Keys.

The four corners of America

The four corners of America all have one thing in common—they look out upon water. Key Largo in Florida has an atmosphere of comfortable loneliness; the small town of Lubec in Maine resembles an outpost on the edge of a virgin frontier; the southwestern corner near San Diego has a backdrop of harsh, dry mountains; and the northwestern corner of America is a peninsula lying beneath the shadow of the striking Olympic Mountains. Northward across the Strait of Juan de Fuca (*above*) is British Columbia. Even in summer, Mt. Olympus wears a thick mantle of snow. Low sea fog is familiar to this country. Along Clallam Bay the country is breath-taking: sharp forest

greens above tumbled rocks along the shoreline. Three
thousand miles eastward is Maine, with some of the most
beautiful coastline in the world. Offshore islands by the
thousands are tree-covered from shore to shore. From
twelve thousand feet they look like green specks floating
on blue water. The sun sets afire the coastal waters with
flashing reflections, and the islands seem to float in a sea
of diamonds. Even the names have the feeling of New England—Handy Boat, Small Point Beach, Cundys Harbor,
Falmouth, Damariscotta, Port Clyde . . . Picturesque coast-
lines and bays lie beneath the mountains of Bar Harbor
and Mt. Desert. Along the coast sheer rock faces loom up
from the water. Just northward, across a narrow inlet, lies
Canada. The coastline is actually the edge of the great
timberland of Maine.

America's exact southwestern edge is unsettled. East of the Ream Naval Air Station (*below*), the small border
community of San Ysidro separates Mexico from the U.S. Maine forests (*right*) near Lubec across the continent.

The many faces of America

Almost lost to sight above an ocean of mountains in western Arizona.

Man, machine and nature

Ghostlike caricatures (*above*) in the wheat fields of the Oregon hills. A herringbone pattern across the ground (*left*) is made by a parking lot of new automobiles in Kenosha, Wisconsin. Nature's mother-of-pearl (*right*); the wave forms of salt in the shoreline pattern of southern Great Salt Lake.

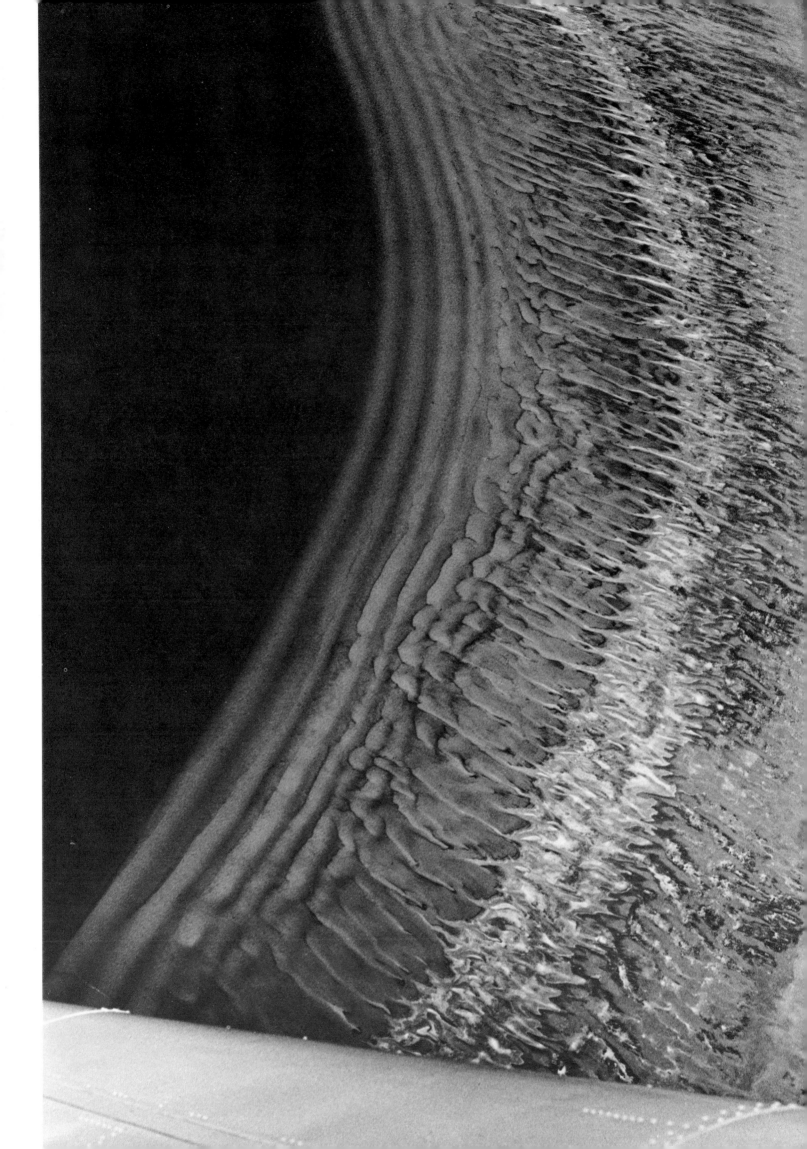

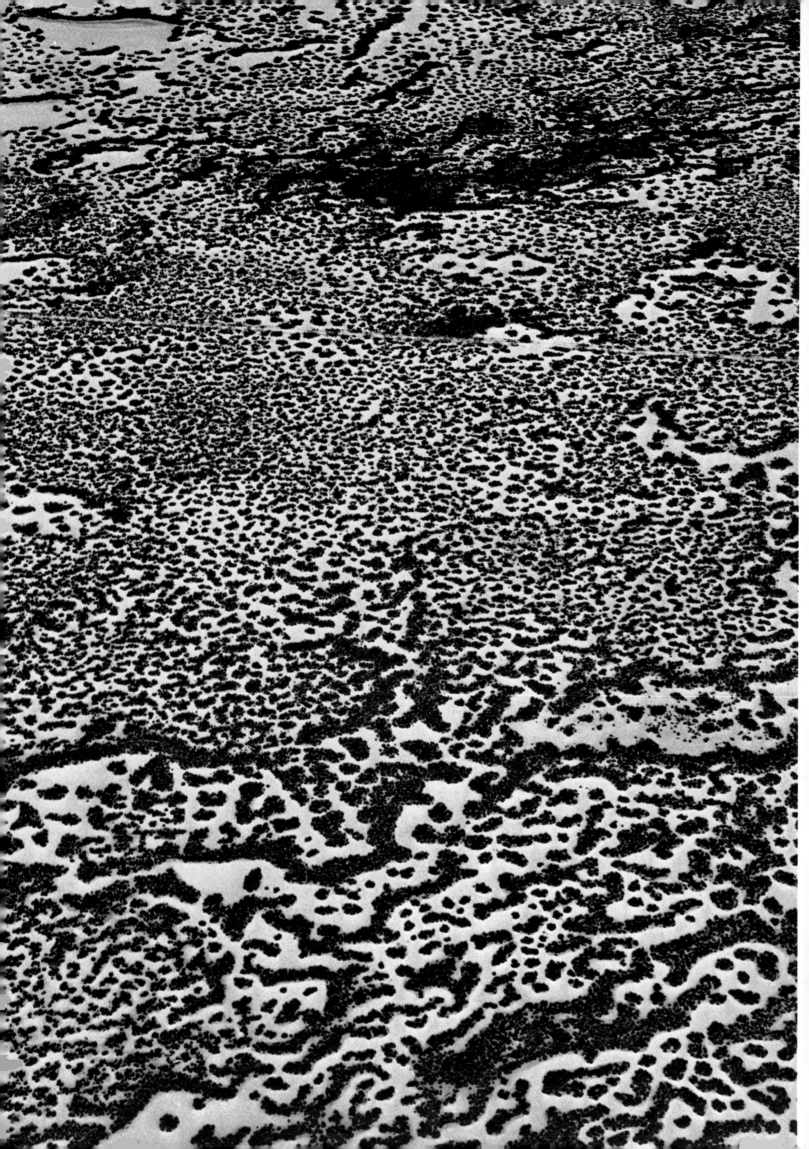

Art gallery

Resembling a laboratory slide, the pattern of the desert in Nevada (*left*) from the air. High over central Virginia (*above*) the veils of wind-blown clouds. The "lightning bolt" (*below*) is deep soil erosion in South Dakota.

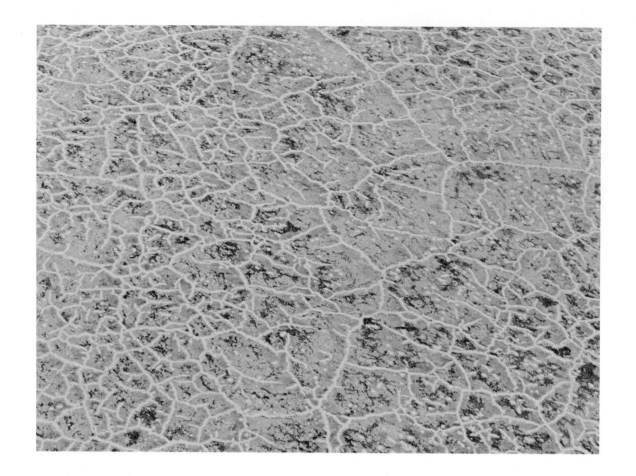

America from the air is a nation of many wonderlands. The mosaic (*above*) might be a marble table cracked into a thousand pieces, instead of the Great Salt Lake Desert in Utah. The strange interplay of lights and shadows (*left*) is formed by a setting sun across the tidewaters of South Carolina's coastline. A strange fairyland (*right*) is beautiful Caddo Lake in Texas. Giant lily pads stand out against the lake's dark waters, which cross the state line into Louisiana. And the skeletal ridges (*far right*) are the result of soil erosion in Utah.

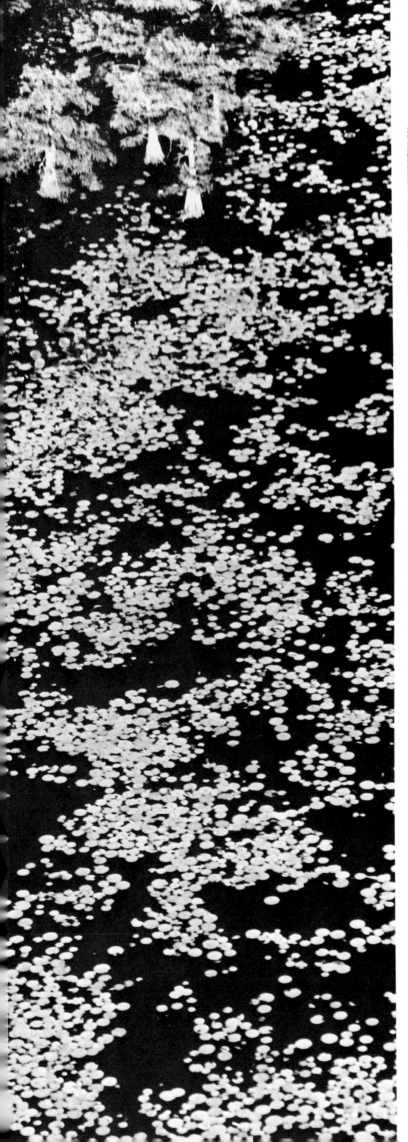

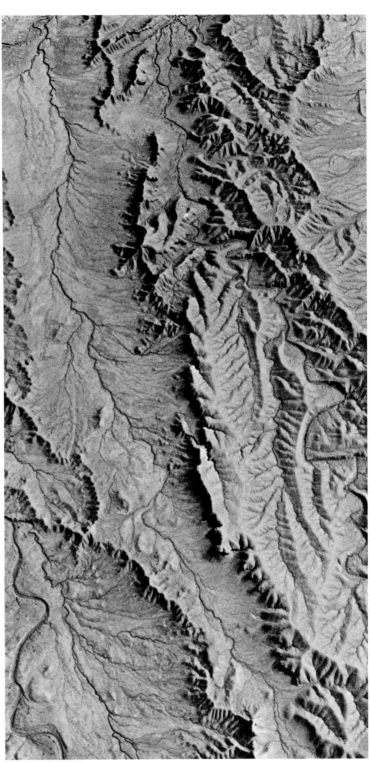

13

The high, rich, flat wheatfields of Montana (*above*) in strip patterns of golden brown.

In North Dakota's rolling hills (*right*), a farmer threshes out a geometric pattern.

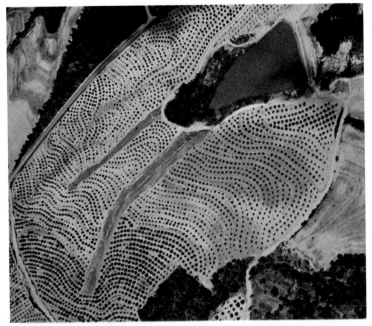

On the ground just an ordinary orchard on a hill, but from above, this North Carolina fruit grove becomes an enormous butterfly.

Farmer's paintbrush

The farmer of America paints the surface of the land in strange, often abstract patterns. His brush is his tractor and reaper, his colors the variety of nature, his canvas the earth.

Date palm groves gleaming brightly at Palm Springs, California.

One of the nation's great highway engineering achievements—the four-level traffic interchange of downtown Los Angeles' Freeway. Criss-crossing pattern comes alive with flashing lights.

16

The touch of man . . .

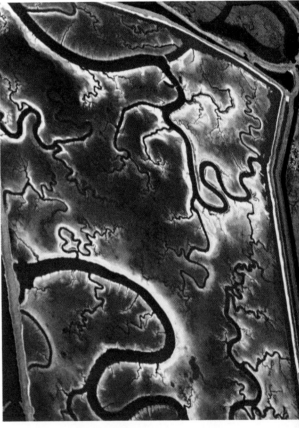

Strip mines (*left*) cut a fabric pattern in the Illinois landscape. Serpentine wanderings of multicolored salt beds (*above*) appear in California's lower San Francisco Bay.

The ceaseless
miracle of
flight

A sapphire burst of dawn above a layer of clouds closely hugging the mountains of Maine (*above*) . . . first light over America.

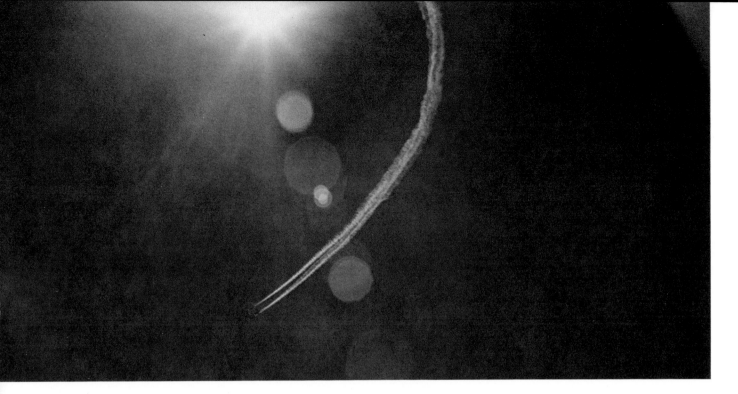

Thunderbirds precision flying team in sky artistry (*above*) over Las Vegas, Nevada. A line of thunderstorms (*below*) near Baton Rouge, Louisiana.

Itinerary for a 55,000-mile visit to America

It began as a dream . . . a visit to and throughout the entire continental United States. Not in just a straight line from one place to another, and not restricted to highways and areas accessible only by road. And not chained to time, either. The dream came true in a summer flight of 58 days and some 55,000 miles of flying. Our *Debonair*—a "magic carpet"—took us from 260 feet below sea level at Death Valley to 16,000 feet above, over the most rug-

ged and hostile terrain in America—where only the vantage of wings makes accessible vast areas of the country. The flight to every state began at Wichita, Kansas, near the geographical center of the country. We looked at the four corners of America, we flew through her valleys, over her rivers, cities, villages, and farms, across her towering mountains, above historic battlefields and trails and her magnificent natural wonders.

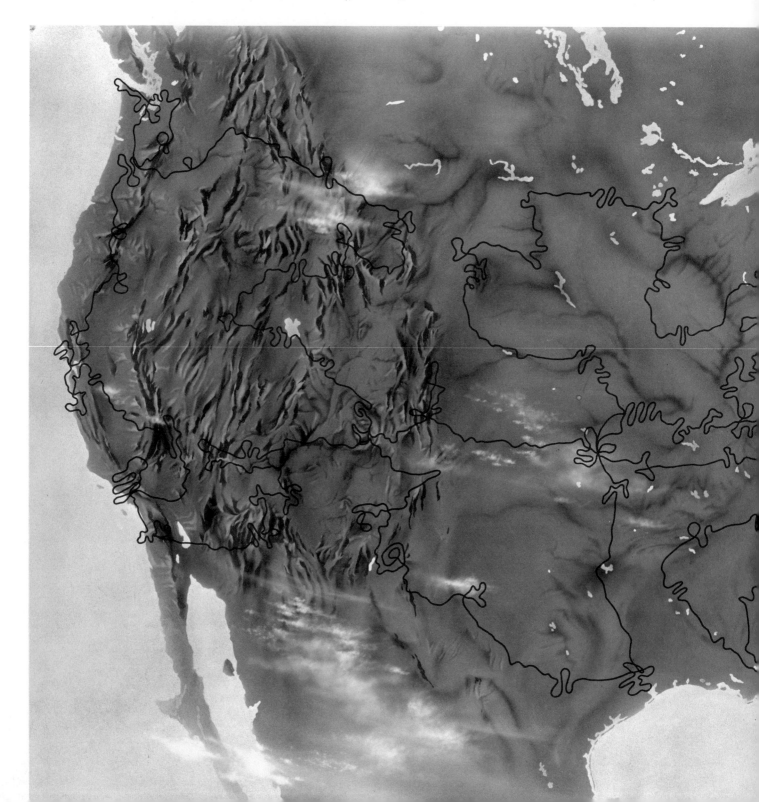

Nine thousand feet over the western shoreline of Lake Mead, not far from Las Vegas.

Great Midwest . . . land

# of bounty

A land where the earth is so rich and well attended that it literally shines beneath the sun . . . this is the Valley of the Red River, lying across the borders of North Dakota and Minnesota.

State lines are artificial boundaries; America from the air has no man-made boundaries by which the sweep of view is separated into carefully defined packages of land. The United States from aloft divides naturally into four great topographical areas: the Great Plains, the Appalachian States, the Lowlands, and the West.

The Great Plains of America are bounded on the west by mountains running north and south (*see map on this page*): the Swan Range, Little and Big Belt Mountains, the Bighorn, Laramie Range, Medicine Bow, Front, Sangre de Cristo and Sacramento Mountains—all part of the Rockies. To the southeast lie the nation's Lowlands, which are less than five hundred feet above sea level. On the east the Great Plains are bounded by the long ridge of the Appalachian Mountains. These plains are the richest, most productive agricultural area of the world. Here the earth's surface is made up of many different patterns: farms that follow hills, forests in rolling blankets of green, and the impressive flatlands of the great wheat and corn belts. Americans work hard to keep this land productive; old strip mines have been heavily seeded to begin the growth of thousands of new trees. Often the gently rolling land is laced with serpentine rivers that appear as green-black threads woven into the earth. In northern Kansas the green patch quilt is replaced with a burnished gold color and enormous farms—dinner table of America.

On this fertile land (*above*) the wheat farmers of Kansas achieve a productivity that astounds the farmers of other countries.

Farmers in South Dakota (*right*) practicing land conservation—planting alternate crops each year. An isolated farm (*far right*) about to receive sudden thunderstorm rains.

THE GREAT PLAINS

A long line of cows ambles home in the late afternoon (*above*); Arkansas River country in western Kansas has many sprawling dairy farms. A farmer in Iowa (*opposite page, top*) paints sweeping curves in the earth, while a Kansas farmer (*opposite page, bottom*) harvests a ruler-straight line of wheat. A South Dakota farmer (*below*) plows a "giant thumbprint" into the soft earth.

Beautiful farm in Iowa, near the Des Moines River.

The old and new combine for prosperity

A circular barn topped with a violet-covered roof in the great dairy state of Wisconsin—Cheeseland, U.S.A.

CHEW
MAIL POUCH
TOBACCO
TREAT YOURSELF TO THE BEST

Southward bound from Indianapolis along Indiana's Highway 31, toward Louisville, Kentucky. Several miles south of Columbia is this delightful sight (*above*), newly painted in bright yellow on an old barn.

Sentinels of the sparsely populated plains are bright, white grain elevators, like this one (*left*) of the Alida Co-op in Kansas.

Contented cows and the ICBM . . .

There are "intruders" in the northern and western areas of the great central plains of the United States. Except for the months when men labor to prepare their installations, their location will be invisible to the eye. The intruders are the giant intercontinental ballistic missiles that are being hidden by the hundreds beneath the soil. The quiet countryside of farms and fields (Wisconsin dairy farm: *below*) is a strange contrast to the subterranean pits and tunnels that will hold the steel rockets.

South of Rapid City, South Dakota (*right*), a line of thunderstorms marches over the ground. Brilliant rainbows arch along the horizon, pointing down to a wound cut far into the surface. Here men are building the deep silos in which the Titan missiles with their hydrogen bomb warheads will be buried. When the work is completed, massive steel doors will cover the rockets.

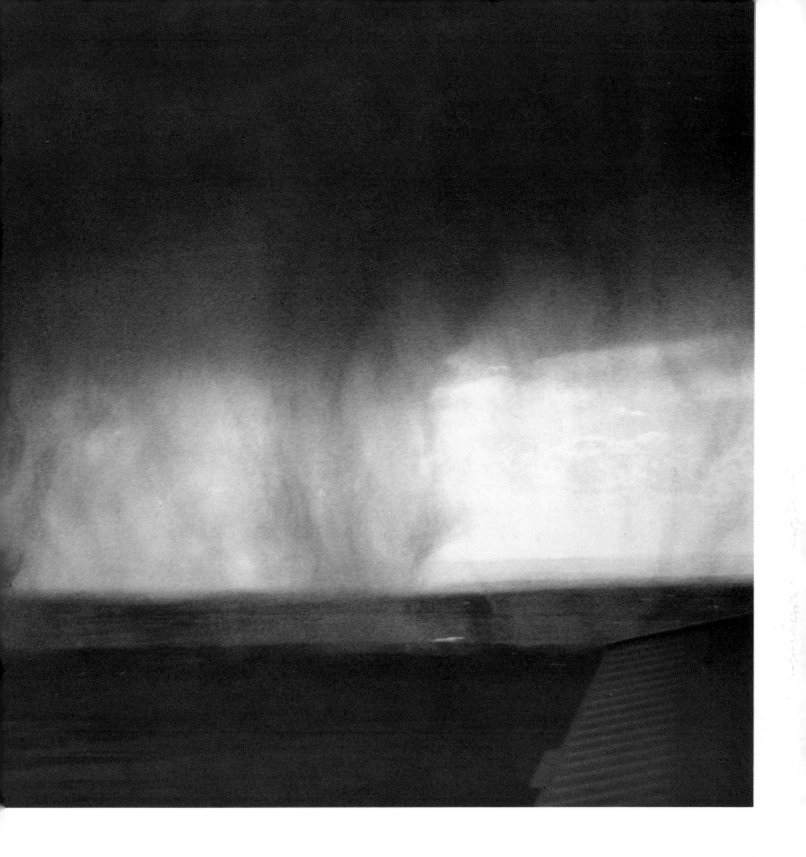

Black angry wall . . .

Over South Dakota's rolling badlands (*left*) a black wall of clouds looms in the distance. Two massive thunderstorms over Nebraska grind together, stabbed by golden sunlight. Then the bottom of the clouds shreds apart (*above*) to pour heavy torrents upon the earth.

Snorting oxen

and roaring Diesels

The first government engineers rode through the country in 1825, peering through instruments and scratching lines on maps to record the surrounding land. This was to be Kansas; and the route was to become famous as the Santa Fe Trail, the great trade pathway stretching 750 miles from the Missouri River to Santa Fe, New Mexico. Five hundred miles of the trail pushed through what would become the richest wheat-growing country in the world. But in those days Kansas' future seemed dim; Pike in 1806 laughed at the thought of people ever living there. Daniel Webster described Kansas as a "vast and worthless area, this region of savages and wild beasts, of deserts of shifting sand and whirlwinds, of dust, of cactus and prairie dogs..." Today, all that remains of the Santa Fe Trail are the scars of wheel ruts (*above*) that the old wagon teams and stolid oxen gouged into the earth. The railroad replaced the trail, and soon a new means of transportation will be this modern superhighway (*right*), seen in its clouds of construction dust.

With a line of impatient drivers running close behind, a huge trailer rig speeds eastward on U.S. 10 (*left*), outward bound from Bismarck, North Dakota, toward Fargo.

Quiet countryside scene in Indiana (*below*); trains run for many miles without any turns.

Enthusiasts of amateur racing roar through a curve (*above*) of race track just north of Rossburg, Indiana.

Roller-coaster road (*below*) through Iowa countryside.

Except for the modern touches of automobiles and fuel tanks, the scene of these side-wheelers (*above*) loading at a Missouri River wharf hasn't changed much from decades past. Along the river bank are small hills and sharp bluffs, with many quiet towns (*below*) resting in the hot summer sun.

The Missouri never changes

Sailing down the Missouri—or drifting lazily above the river—is a wonderful way to spend an afternoon. Jefferson City is like an old storybook page coming to life. Missouri towns still hear the booming whistles of the steamboats; the kids still navigate the river in homebuilt rafts.

40

Industry and the atom

The south shore of Lake Michigan is lined with scores of America's greatest industries. Row upon row of steel mills stretch for miles, like the great complex (*above left*) at Gary, Indiana. The earth blinks with the light of open fires, and from the buildings pour streamers of multicolored smoke (*left*). The old industry has been joined today by a new and quiet source of energy; an atomic power plant (*above*) at Dresden, Illinois.

Arrow-shaped wedges of stacked boards (*left*) in a lumbermill at Texarkana, Texas.

Land of lakes, farms, great dairy herds—Minnesota is also the leading state in iron ore production. To support these and other industries, St. Paul marshaling yards (*right*) process freight cars leading to all America.

Tile kilns of a large factory (*above*) at Texarkana. The city is a vigorous industrial center on the Texas-Arkansas border.

Flying over Rapid City, South Dakota, there appeared in the distance a field of glittering lights. Low over the ground, the lights became a graveyard (*right*) for old autos—useless junk for the driver but vital raw materials for the production of steel goods.

Mt. Rushmore—where four great men of our nation
gaze eternally upon the rolling plains and mountains.

Tribute to a nation . . .

Historians say that "a sense of time hangs heavy in the Black Hills of South Dakota." To students of the earth's history the Black Hills are a geological diary of eons past. Scientists come here from all over the world to unearth fossils preserved here for countless centuries; and they talk of dinosaurs, of saber-toothed tigers, and of giant creatures that more than sixty million years ago swam in the sea where a city now stands. These hills create one of America's most memorable sights, with their high buttresses carved by time and weather. They are best known for Mt. Rushmore, upon whose face are carved the magnificent sculptures of four great men of America—George Washington, Thomas Jefferson, Theodore Roosevelt, and Abraham Lincoln. Geologists predict that this monumental work of the sculptor Gutzon Borglum will still be here one hundred thousand years from now.

Beautiful Minnesota

Blue lakes and rich forests . . . this is Minnesota.

Otis Lodge at Sugar Lake (above) near Grand Rapids,
Minnesota. The golf course makes a perfect runway.

Loneliness of the plains and crowded mining towns . . .

Years ago this hilltop community (*right*) of Lead, South Dakota, boomed with a gold rush. The rush is gone, the Western heroes are dusty memories, but the gold is still there. Lead is the site of the famed Homestake Mine, greatest producer of gold in the country—and the world's fourth greatest source of gold. More than one hundred miles of tunneled underground chambers for small railway cars honeycomb the earth.

48

Flanking the northeastern edge of the Black Hills of South Dakota, Bear Butte (*above*) stands vigil over the plains beyond. In the old pioneer days the Fourth Cavalry rode out from Fort Meade through this country to fight some of the bloodiest Indian battles in our history.

A line through the center of this photograph of the Red River takes you from Texas (*bottom*) to Oklahoma to Texas and back to Oklahoma—in a straight flight of only four minutes.

From aloft Madison, Wisconsin, is one of the most attractive of America's cities. Surrounded by three lakes and lined with trees, Madison seems like "the right kind of a city for settling down."

Cities of the Midwest

Few cities present the neat, carefully planned appearance of Indianapolis (left), capital of Indiana. Well known for its annual racing classic at the Indianapolis Speedway, the city is the center of the nation's fastest growing industrial state.

The city of Hannibal, Missouri (right), where Mark Twain's home has become a museum, and a whitewashed fence brings back memories of Tom Sawyer and Huckleberry Finn.

"K.C." . . . just great!

There are still "nomads" among us. In America, trailer living is a vigorous part of our way of life. Perched atop a high hill in Rapid City, South Dakota (left), is this neat grouping of large trailers, each fenced in precisely to create its own homesite.

A striped biplane (above) dashes low across Minneapolis, Minnesota, as the pilot swoops to spray chemicals onto the city's trees.

Clean and crisp in the morning, Kansas City, Missouri, begins a sparkling summer day (left). Kansas City Municipal Airport is so close to the downtown business district that its citizens are accustomed to airliners drifting past their windows as they land.

The Nebraska state capitol in Lincoln. Atop the four-hundred-foot tower is a bronze statue of the Sower—casting forth seed as a fitting symbol of this state's vast wheat and corn industry.

...Biggest Little City

Midland, Texas ... from the center of this small city rises an assembly of modern office buildings (*above*), structures of which Dallas, Tulsa or Manhattan would be proud. The penitentiary at Joliet, Illinois (*left*), a grim, walled-in "city within a city."

Wichita, Kansas, glows softly in the night. The industrial complex of Beech Aircraft in Wichita was "home" to our *Debonair*. Beech, along with Cessna Aircraft, make Wichita the world's leading producer of modern business airplanes.

Deadwood, South Dakota (*above*). In this town's Mount Moriah Cemetery lie the remains of Wild Bill Hickok, Preacher Smith, Calamity Jane, Potato Creek Johnny and other improbably named but very real characters of the Old West. The Kansas community of Dodge City (*below*), made famous in years past by Wyatt Earp, Bat and Ed Masterson, "Doc" Holiday and other gunmen. Today, Dodge City is a thriving transportation and industrial center, typified by high white grain elevators along its railroad.

Hemmed in and crowded on all sides, the small gray chapel and some courtyard walls of the Alamo—center foreground—are all that remain of the famed fortress and mission. Davy Crockett, Jim Bowie and other pioneers of America's frontier days died here in the defense of the Alamo against an overwhelming Mexican attack. The modern city of San Antonio, Texas, has spread outward and now completely surrounds this honored national shrine.

Along Chicago's lake front (*opposite page*), is Meigs Field, that permits flying businessmen to be in the heart of the Loop within ten minutes of landing. To the left of the airport is Soldier Field; at the airport's upper right corner is Adler Planetarium. Looking at the Loop (*left*) from the southwest, and (*below*) at a large fleet of cabin cruisers, sailboats, yachts in the water basin between Meigs Field and the shoreline.

Chicago . . .
city of the unexpected, hub of a continent

Lakes make a
Midwestern playground

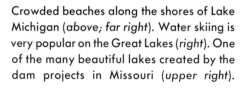
Crowded beaches along the shores of Lake Michigan (*above; far right*). Water skiing is very popular on the Great Lakes (*right*). One of the many beautiful lakes created by the dam projects in Missouri (*upper right*).

Land of black gold . . .

The vast oil fields of Texas' Permian Basin . . .

A land rich in oil; thirsting for water. A water hole in West Texas.

Texas' statistics are impressive. The Permian Basin oil fields are an example of the state's thriving industry that produces forty percent of the oil and fifty percent of the natural gas for the entire United States. Across the desert floor of West Texas, the thousands of oil and gas wells surround scattered refineries like this installation (*left*), that lies on a small road between Andrews, Texas, and Eunice, New Mexico. Thirty miles from Andrews is Midland, headquarters for more than six hundred oil firms.

Oil Town: U.S.A.

A thriving modern city and transportation center, Tulsa in Oklahoma is also called the "financial center" of the American oil industry. Refineries and storage tanks (*above*) extend along the south shores of the Arkansas River; Tulsa center lies to the north.

Gateway to America . . .

Rich in history, powerful with industry, blessed with beauty . . .

No one section of America is so rich in history, industry, or geographical diversity as the Appalachian Ridge States. The topographical features of the country clearly delineate this area, which includes all of New England—Maine, Vermont, Massachusetts, New Hampshire, Connecticut and Rhode Island; the Central Northeast—New York, New Jersey, Pennsylvania, West Virginia, and, because of their proximity, Delaware, Maryland and the District of Columbia; and in the Central East and South—sections of Ken-

tucky, Virginia, Tennessee, North Carolina and the northern edges of Alabama and Virginia. The Appalachian Ridge, running in a northeast-southwest line, includes the Cumberland Plateau, the Allegheny and Blue Ridge Mountains, the Catskills and the Adirondacks. It embraces the Statue of Liberty, symbol of the gateway to America, in New York Harbor (*left*) as well as the Ozarks, where much of the land remains as primitive as when hunters and pioneers saw it many decades ago.

THE APPALACHIAN RIDGE STATES

Magic city

World center of trade and commerce, capital of countless industries, home of the United Nations, New York also symbolizes travel to all the world. The *Queen Mary* (*right*) departs for Europe. Manhattan (*opposite page*) is known above all for its unmatched office buildings, over which towers (*above*) the antenna-topped one-hundred-and-two-story Empire State building.

The mighty George Washington Bridge—
after sunset it becomes a double-strand
necklace of glowing blue-green lights.

The United Nations Building along midtown Manhattan's East River Drive.

Yankee Stadium in the Bronx (*above*), looking toward Manhattan
Miles to the south, along the shipping piers on Manhattan's west
side, tugs ease a Panama Line freighter (*right*) into the Hudson River

Uptown—Downtown

Long Island is crisscrossed with a constantly growing network of parkways (*above*) and expressways for a mushrooming population. At Southern State Parkway's toll booth (*below*) in light traffic.

Long Island . . .
tied to New York's apron strings

Not so many years ago an area of open spaces and great estates, the flatlands of Long Island (*above*) have been transformed into massive housing areas—like this symmetrical expansion of family cubicles at Levittown, where every family proudly owns its own home. Here a steadily increasing standard of living coupled with homes of lower prices built through new mass-production methods created a new type of American suburbia.

More than 2,400 acres of beautiful beach make up the Jones Beach State Park on the Atlantic Ocean shoreline of Nassau County in Long Island (*right*). At night the high tower is visible to ships many miles out to sea.

Up along the coastline

A sheltered harbor beneath forested hills . . . Bar Harbor, Maine.

Like a page sliced neatly out of New England history—Edgartown on the island of Martha's Vineyard, off Massachusetts.

At the edge of the forests

Pennsylvania means heavy industry to many people; they forget the great forest sections of the state. But here industry and nature can go hand in hand, as with these power lines (*left*) that arrow through the wooded hills of central Pennsylvania. The harbor of Gloucester, Massachusetts (*right*), snug and picturesque. The renowned Gloucester fishermen are considered the most "closely knit" fishing fleet in the United States.

The countryside of Vermont has been described as a "perfect harmony of man and nature, of villages and hills," and is typified by this tiny village (*above*) near Burlington and Lake Champlain.

Notes from a diary: "As we continue our flight beneath the clouds along the wild, lake-dotted north woods of Maine, we are impressed anew by the enormous size of the country, and by its vast stretches of virgin land. We are really not so far from Boston, yet this country is a wilderness with few inhabitants. For mile after mile the great forests roll on, green and beautiful. As hundreds of lakes, large and small, slip beneath our wings, we can see on the shores bear, deer, and many moose."

Fabulous timberland

Notes from a diary: "The dawn of a new day over the woods of Maine (*above*), with logging operations well under way. In the lakes and waterways are great fields of logs. Sometimes they form a pear-shaped pattern as a powerful boat tugs another mass of wood toward the mills along the lake shores at Millinocket, Maine (*right*). Low over the ground an old yellow-painted biplane dusted the woods with a thin spray of chemicals. Then it darted over the town, looking like a yellow dragonfly in the morning sun. The logs are always plentiful in the lakes; they remain in water sometimes as long as three years before mill delivery, so that the bark will slip off naturally."

Mt. Whiteface (*above*), at Lake Placid, New York. At this famous all-year resort and sports center, athletes from many countries meet for training and Olympic competition. Fort Ticonderoga (*below*) in New York State is carefully maintained to look the way it did originally. Among the men who fought here for American independence was Ethan Allen. In 1766 Benedict Arnold used the fort as headquarters to assemble our first battle fleet. A wooden-covered bridge (*right*) at Reading, Pennsylvania.

Horseshoe Falls of mighty Niagara Falls. These are the falls on Canada's side of the Niagara River; they form a great curving horseshoe with a crest extending more than a half-mile in width. Niagara Falls are visited by more tourists than any other scenic wonder in the United States. Late in the day, a freighter (*right*) on Lake Erie near Buffalo Harbor, New York.

Mecca for
industry
and tourists

America is a land of interconnecting highways and steel railways. Sometimes these transportation ribbons rush together (*left*) to span a river—like these bridges crossing the Mississippi at Memphis, Tennessee.

Although Maryland and Delaware are two of the smallest states in land area, their combined industrial strength has become a force (linked with the heavy industry of New York, New Jersey and Pennsylvania) known as the American Ruhr. Steel mills and shipyards (*below*) along Maryland's coast.

The Genesee River bisects the heart of the "photographic capital of the world"—Rochester, New York (*above*), on Lake Ontario's south shoreline.

The rolling green farms and forests of the Tennessee Valley.

A country of green

The broad and fertile valley of the Cumberland River (*right*), near the city of Nashville, Tennessee. A horse farm (*left*), near the Atlantic coastline of the state of Delaware.

High above the river

In 1889 the South Fork Dam at the end of Conemaugh Valley, Pennsylvania, split open. "With a noise like that of a thousand thunderbolts," a wall of black water plunged down the valley into Johnstown. The sudden flood claimed 2,205 lives. Today, in Grandview Cemetery overlooking Johnstown, 777 unidentified victims lie in the "Unknown Plot."

Air Force troop carrier planes aligned in symmetrical neatness (*above*) at Nashville, Tennessee. "Cotton puffballs" curve over a hill (*below*) in this orchard lying west of Buffalo, New York.

Out of the man-made mists . . .

Industrial smoke, natural haze, and low-lying levels of cold air produce heavy smog for many cities. One community that has worked hard, and successfully, to eliminate this problem is Pittsburgh, Pennsylvania (*below*).

Haze hugs the earth (*left*) in West Virginia's "Smokies."

Notes from a diary: "From 14,000 feet the sun's rays slanting through the haze against the city and the wooded countryside make it seem as if Pittsburgh lies beneath eddying waters. Then, closer to earth, the city's Golden Triangle becomes clear and sharp to the eye. Commanding attention is the tower of the University of Pittsburgh. Eighteen bridges, large and small, cross the rivers. And cable cars, like ants on a hill, creep slowly along."

Steel towers . . . and water in suburbia

Notes from a diary: "In the early morning sunlight, the city of Nashville, Tennessee, stands out crisply against the green countryside. Suddenly, from within the suburban section of Nashville, a flash of light appeared on the ground. Looming huge against neighboring homes was a great circular dam of water (*left*) in the heart of a residential section. Bisecting the dam was a broad walkway—with a brilliant-red two-story house."

Narrow streets and chowder

A labyrinth of twisting streets, Old Boston is the site of great moments in the birth of the United States. There are "several Bostons," old and new. In the busy water-front area (*left*) rises the sharp white spire of Old North Church, where Paul Revere received his famous "One if by land, two if by sea" lantern signals. High above the city looms the new skyscraper courthouse (*above*); a scene in residential Boston (*below*).

Rivers and canals make the towns and cities . . .

Few inland communities have ever demonstrated so effectively as Pittsburgh, Pennsylvania, that "rivers and canals make the towns and cities." Lying along the western side of the Alleghenies, where the Monongahela and Allegheny Rivers meet to form the Ohio, Pittsburgh began its history originally as Fort Duquesne, and then, Fort Pitt. After an early career of bloody battles with the French and the British, it began to flourish as a key trading post. The Northwest Territory was nourished through Pittsburgh, and commerce for communities along the Ohio River was encouraged by growing industry and shipping facilities. Finally the city grew into the mighty industrial giant we know today—the world's greatest producer of iron and of steel.

New York State's Erie Canal—ridiculed as "Clinton's Ditch" (*above*) when it was built in 1825—proved the key to the future wealth of the state. The canal is still heavily traveled by barges.

Symbols of summer vacation and sailing pleasures, boats fleck the waters (*above*) off Rhode Island's coastline, mecca for marine enthusiasts.

The Lowlands of America . . .

A forbidding expanse of cypress swamps, shallow water, and saw grass morasses—the Florida Everglades. At lower left is wreckage of an airplane.

Water-front home at Melbourne, mideastern Florida.

A primeval land
where man is the intruder

As the name implies, the Lowlands of America comprise the lowest topographical area of the nation. Except for some isolated hill country, at no point do the Lowlands reach higher than five hundred feet above sea level. As the topographical map of the United States shows (*below*), the Lowlands extend from the southeastern edge of the Great Plains to the Gulf Coast and the Atlantic shoreline. The Lowlands include all of Louisiana, Mississippi and Florida; most of Alabama, Georgia, South Carolina, North Carolina, and Virginia; parts of Texas, Arkansas, and Missouri; and the edges of Illinois, Indiana, Kentucky, and Tennessee. The Atlantic coast north of Virginia also includes, topographically, part of the Lowlands, but because of the influence of the communities, they are included in the Appalachian States.

THE LOWLANDS

Two houseboats and a floating pier nestle among the trees and foliage of Caddo Lake in Texas. The water is a deep blue, overlaid with brilliantly colored lily pads in clusters. (*Below*) Eerie vistas of Everglades south of Lake Okeechobee in rainstorm.

The bayou country of the Mississippi River Delta (*above*), south of New Orleans. Boat hulks (*below*) on bayou waterway sandbar.

Where nature
and man
live together

Low clouds in the late afternoon (*above*), near Baton Rouge, Louisiana. (*Left*) White herons in the Louisiana bayous of the Mississippi River Delta. This is one of the greatest bird and game preserves in America.

Tidewaters and floating coastal rigs for oil

The southern half of the Atlantic coastline is both varied and beautiful. For many miles, without interruption, the white beaches sharply delineate the land from the ocean. At times the white sand ends abruptly, to be replaced with flat expanses of green and brown tidewater swamps that ex- tend well inland, like this scene (*left*) in South Carolina. Oil rigs (*above*) tower from the waters of Goose Creek, alongside the fifty-mile Ship Channel of Houston, Texas. One of the country's most dynamic cities, Houston is also our third busiest seaport.

Variety from the earth

Rice fields (*left*) in Arkansas.

Virginia farm (*above*) against a border of heavily forested areas.

A sweeping curve of tobacco fields and neat orchards in the Georgia countryside (*left*). Near the town of Moultrie, Georgia, are forests of tall and thin pines (*below*), used for lumber and for telephone poles.

Ten thousand feet over the
patch-quilt blanket of North
Carolina's fields and farms
(left). Along the Florida
coastline, great cumulus
clouds (right) build up during the early afternoon

A countryside of green and a canopy of clouds (*above*)—summertime along the Arkansas River, near Little Rock in Arkansas.

North of Atlanta, Georgia, lies the huge gray form of Stone Mountain (*above*). The Civil War's bloody Battle of Stone Mountain was fought around its slopes.

Rolling hills with long rows of orchards and groves—morning in Virginia (*left*).

A Nation remembers . . .

In 1775 the Second Virginia Convention met in Richmond at St. John's Church (*left*) in an attempt to avert war with England. Among the group of patriots assembled in the white frame structure on Church Hill was the country lawyer, Patrick Henry. Weary of futile attempts to obtain justice for the Colonists, he rose in his pew to demand the immediate arming of the Virginia militia. Then came the words that ignited the flames of Revolution and made possible this nation: "Is life so dear, or peace so sweet, as to be purchased at the price of chains and slavery? Forbid it, Almighty God! I know not what course others may take, but, as for me, give me liberty or give me death!" (*Above*) Surrounded by tall trees, the home of Thomas Jefferson, just beyond Charlottesville, Virginia.

The guns of Vicksburg, Mississippi (*above*), on the high bluffs of the city stand in their original positions, reminders of the city's fierce battles fought during its siege and defense in 1863.

"That the future may learn from the past," is the theme of Colonial Williamsburg in Virginia, the most exacting restoration in the country. More than four hundred buildings in an area a mile long and almost half as wide are kept as they appeared in the eighteenth century. Williamsburg was the meeting place for the men who helped create our nation—such as George Washington, Patrick Henry, Thomas Jefferson.

Standing out clearly against the backdrop of Montgomery (*above*) are the capitol and other government buildings of Alabama. On the front portico of the capitol building, Jefferson Davis in 1861 took his oath of office as the first Confederate President.

Moored permanently in Buffalo Bayou on the edge of San Jacinto Battleground near Houston, Texas, is the old battleship *Texas* (*left*), a veteran of a dozen campaigns fought in two world wars, and the only survivor of the dreadnought-class of warships.

117

A way of life

White-columned plantation homes of the South in Louisiana and Mississippi, like this lovely structure (*above*) near Natchez, form a long line on both sides of the Mississippi River. Many years ago they represented the hub about which wheeled great agricultural empires of the nation. For the most part the vast sugar-cane and cotton holdings have been broken up into smaller farms. But the plantation homes remain a part of the South's own way of life—as weekend estates or as the residence of people who live in quiet seclusion. Homes that are entirely different are these crowded, colorful buildings of New Orleans' French Quarter (*left*). And the most famous—as well as the largest—stern-wheeler ever built is the huge *Sprague* (*below*). Riverboat men talk about the *Sprague* with affection: "We love her, but she's absolutely hell on wheels to handle in the river."

Summer solitude . . .

Tucked away on a quiet side road, yellow school buses (*above*) wait out the fishing and swimming season. The beautiful Town Square (*right*) of Moultrie, Georgia. (*Below*) A neat and immaculately kept residential section in the city of Charleston, South Carolina.

Mouth of the delta

"By all the laws of nature," a merchant captain once said, "New Orleans just shouldn't be." The city of New Orleans (*above*) lies on land that is only five feet higher than the mean level of the Gulf of Mexico. Despite the danger of storms and tides, New Orleans is the largest city in Louisiana, one of the greatest commercial distributing centers of the South, and a leading port of the United States. New Orleans is best known, however, for its French Quarter, Bourbon Street, and for the most spectacular festival—the Mardi Gras—of the entire country. The most unusual land grants to be found in the United States (*right*) are these thin, long slices of farms in the Mississippi River Delta. They originated in the time of strict land control by governing France officials.

Of all the areas of the Lowlands and the South, none has exhibited such rapid growth as Florida's Atlantic coastline. The southern beach communities are known as part of the Gold Coast. Only seventy-five years ago Miami Beach and the cities northward were a wilderness of swamps and bogs, of palmetto thickets and mangrove forests—inhabited by wildcats, bear, snakes, deer, alligators and great flocks of birds. In the Cape Canaveral area, despite the flame and thunder of giant rockets, the Florida coastline remains one of the country's best bird sanctuaries.

Row upon row of private homes along the south Florida coast—the Gold Coast (*below*). A sweeping panorama of Greater Miami (*right*) and artificial islands created along the slim causeways.

Cities of the Lowlands

A new superhighway (*above*) during construction in Jacksonville, Florida. Large factory (*below*) near Little Rock, Arkansas.

Tobacco Road—contemporary style (*above*): factories along the Main Street of Richmond, Virginia, tobacco center of the world.

Rising from the edge of the Mississippi River to high bluffs (*right*), the countryside of Vicksburg, Mississippi, is filled with ravines, caves, and thick, tangled undergrowth.

Oil, skyscrapers, and parking lots

The eighth largest city in America, booming with new industry and factories, Houston, Texas, is confident that in the next several decades its population will soar to at least three million people. Houston today is one of the great seaports of the world, serviced by a fifty-mile Ship Channel (*above*), the shores of which are lined with many industrial plants. This economic and industrial bastion of the West was founded by two New Yorkers, the Allen Brothers; in 1836 they launched a major newspaper campaign to sell townsites along Buffalo Bayou, prophesying that Houston was certain to become "the great interior commercial emporium of Texas." Downtown Houston (*right*) seems to have more space for parking its many thousands of automobiles than it does for the modern office buildings needed to handle its business.

View to the west of Miami Beach, overlooking the artificial islands.

Florida Gold Coast

The beautiful clubs, marinas and luxurious homes of Florida's Gold Coast—an area of beaches and meticulously kept waterways.

On July 24, 1950, the United States Air Force fired the first rocket ever launched from Cape Canaveral. The nearby town of Cocoa Beach (*below*), lying a dozen miles to the south, had a population of just over two hundred people. Today, twelve years later, Cape Canaveral has become a true port for the new ships of space—and the population of Cocoa Beach is ten thousand persons, and still growing. Now a fresh excitement is in the air. At Cape Canaveral (the upper far right of the picture), work has already begun on the launching sites from which, in the near future, we will send an Apollo spaceship to the moon.

THE MAGNIFICENT

MONUMENT VALLEY, UTAH

WEST

A world of gods and men

Notes from a diary: "Garden of the Gods at Manitou Springs, Colorado, is a breathtaking sight. The red rock formations look as if they were sculptured by hand. They are flecked with gold and spattered with green. Rock pinnacles loom upward like obelisks. Razorlike ridges are balanced precariously along their sides; from above, the ridges are so thin that the long, wide shadows they cast are startling. There are spires, and angled formations, and pedestals, and they seem to change their shapes when viewed from different sides. The Garden of the Gods is aptly named; there is not another place in America quite like this."

(*Below*) "From eighty miles away and fourteen thousand feet high, Monument Valley, extending from Utah into Arizona, is clearly defined. Nature has created here an enormous amphitheater strewn with needlelike crags and rows of thin high rock, with buttes and mesas, and massive columns that tower upward for hundreds of feet. It seems to be an alien surface—not of this world of earth—where time stands still."

...reate new lands

THE WEST

The mountain deserts of southern Nevada and northern Arizona, even after the turn of the century, were so isolated and barren that only the most determined prospectors settled in the area for any length of time. It would have remained barren except for a dream of skilled engineers . . . a dream of a great dam that would back up the waters of the Colorado River and bring new life to the desert. More than thirty years ago the formidable task began. The engineers, using dynamite, blasted four tunnels through Black Canyon to divert the Colorado River. Then they sliced grooves deep into the sides of the canyon. The wall of the dam began to rise high above the canyon floor. With power drills and more dynamite the engineers blasted ninety-one tunnels through solid rock to control flood waters. When they were through, Hoover Dam rose 727 feet from the canyon bottom. The dam stopped, and then pushed back, the Colorado River. Finally there stretched across the desert floor beautiful Lake Mead with a shoreline of more than five hundred miles. Not since the day Hoover Dam was completed has the Colorado caused a dangerous flood, and tens of thousands of square miles of desert land have been opened to settlers because of the light and power produced by the dam's generators. Where water once was scarce, it is now plentiful, because some men once nourished a dream, and brought it to reality.

(On following page) Soaring in toward Wyoming's citadels—the Grand Tetons.

Mighty

Columbia and "Les Trois Tetons"

The mighty Columbia River (*left*) in Oregon. When all the dams that engineers plan one day to build are stretched across its waters, the area will draw from this river as much electrical energy as can be produced by *all* of America's other natural sources of power. The saw-toothed peaks (*above*) of Wyoming's Grand Tetons, considered by many as our most beautiful mountains.

Lowest point in America . . .

Notes from a diary: "At the southern end of Death Valley are low, rounded mountains (*above*), which stand as the last ground barrier to the north. These stone hills drifted to the side and then behind the airplane as our altitude dropped steadily; then came the strange sensation of flight *below* sea level. Death Valley is unexpectedly colorful, with the valley floor and walls streaked with red, green, white, brown, and gray. Along the western edge, sparse groups of trees and bushes cling to life. The desert floor changes constantly. Sometimes it appears as a swirl of colors and patterns (*right*). When the heavy rains in the mountains send water cascading into the valley, the water leaves behind serpentine markings. There are great flat expanses of baked mud, and many strange designs. And there are the sand dunes, brilliant and carved neatly by the wind, their shapes changing from month to month."

Death Valley

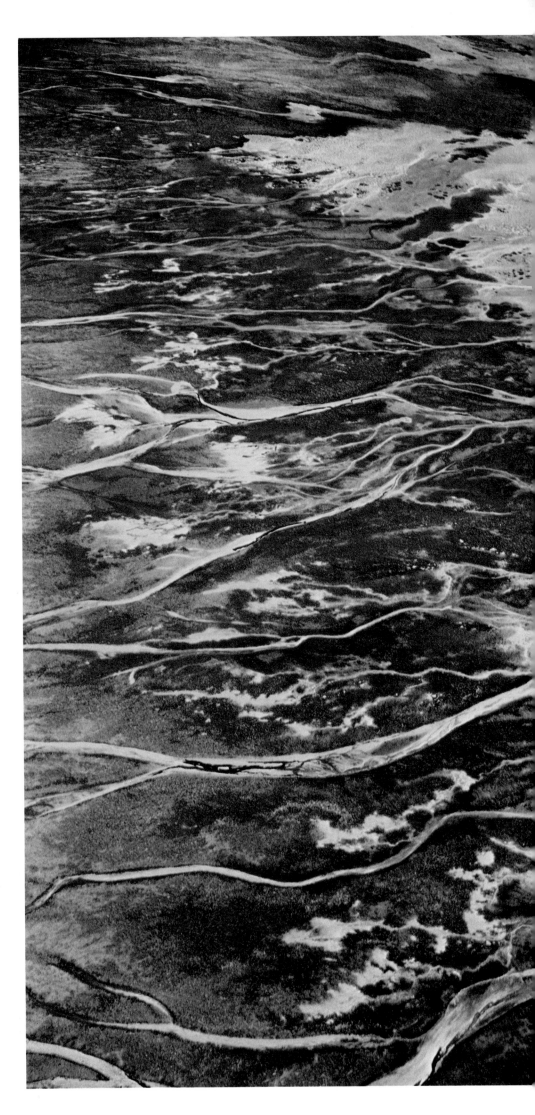

A valley of
stark contrasts

The flat, blistered earth of Death Valley (*below*) stretches to the foot of flanking mountains. Besides the baked earth, the alkali beds and serpentine patterns, there are also ridged sand dunes (*right*), where the temperature can sometimes reach 135° F.

Among the more grotesque works of nature are these Craters of the Moon, in Idaho. The surface is of black lava that has solidified into many weird patterns.

The Craters of the Moon are not entirely lifeless. In some places sturdy desert plants have dug into the lava, and their green stands out against the black.

A land where
fire once ran

This Arizona cinder cone was "alive" only a thousand years ago.

In geological terms the western part of the United States is a land of many "young" volcanoes. Throughout the mountain states there are literally hundreds of large cinder cones and volcanic peaks. Some of them, especially in California, have sent fiery lava streams down their sides since the turn of the century. The area surrounding Humphreys Peak in Arizona, near Flagstaff, is overrun with cinder cones and black lava beds. Many of these peaks and cones cannot be seen from the ground. From aloft, however, the lava streams are easily visible, and the courses once taken by these burning rivers stand out clearly. Miles to the south and southeast of Flagstaff, beyond the thick wooded hills, the country is almost a continuous, rolling desert zone of cones and lava beds.

From the upper ridges of Colorado's Sangre de Cristo Mountains, a great plateau stretches to the west. Here is one of America's greatest natural wonders . . . a mass of high sand dunes whose brilliance is almost painful to the eyes. These are the Great Sand Dunes of Colorado, more than a thousand feet in depth and rising nearly two miles above sea level.

Lofty desert, magic river

This unusual river flows at the edge of the Great Sand Dunes. It vanishes deep into the ground—to reappear many miles away.

Fire gods and devil's tower

Meteor Crater in Arizona (*above*) is a great circular scar in the earth visible from many miles away, the aftermath of a single meteorite that struck the earth at many thousands of miles per hour. An explosion of another kind—when a giant volcano collapsed within itself—created beautiful Crater Lake (*right*) in the Cascade Range of Oregon. The color of Crater Lake is so deep that it is called the "bluest blue" ever known. At Missouri Butte in Wyoming rears Devil's Tower (*upper right*). Falcons and hawks, and other birds, make their nests atop its flat peak.

Near Santa Fe, New Mexico, a sudden summer thunderstorm (*above*) moves rapidly over the countryside. Bright sun and heavy rains (*below*) create this beautiful scene along a Wyoming mountain range. And stretched over the mountains of Idaho (*right*) are these unusual markings, looking like a green-striped tiger pelt across the earth.

A variety
of
homesteads

Deep inside a remote area of the Grand Canyon there is a "Garden of Eden." In the midst of the barren gorge there suddenly appears a thin river, neat farms and buildings (*left*)— this is home for the Havasupai Indians.

Nestled deep within Red Mountain Pass of the towering San Juan Mountains of Colorado is the little settlement (*left*) of Silverton.

Lying in the shadow of California's San Jacinto Peak is Palm Springs (*above*), a vacation mecca surrounded by barren desert.

The tortured earth . . .

The American West is a scene of constant change. The Grand Canyon is famed throughout the world, but the West has many lesser-known features which deserve the visitor's attention, such as this serpentine gorge in Utah (*right*), that stands out clearly from above. These brightly colored cliffs (*below*) and ravines of wide Oak Creek Canyon, which winds through Arizona, create one of the most unusual natural formations in America.

The *Debonair* passes over the town of Acoma (*above*) in New Mexico. Acoma—its name means "Sky City"—is the oldest continuously inhabited community in America. There is little doubt that it was settled for many decades before the first white explorers (Coronado in 1540) ever reached New Mexico. Southwest of Colorado Springs (*right*) is the world's highest suspension bridge—crossing the Royal Gorge, with the Arkansas River 1,053 feet below. At Bingham, Utah (*below*), is the world's greatest open-pit copper mine, which looks like a great man-made coliseum.

Against a backdrop of "islands from a Japanese print," a filmy sandbar floats out into Great Salt Lake, Utah.

A mushroom once grew here

The ridges of the Sierra Oscura Mountains and the San Andres Range were still dark on the morning of July 16, 1945. Suddenly, in this quiet valley bed between the shielding peaks, there blazed a light of unbelievable brilliance. Miles away, Georgia Green, a young blind girl, cried out: *"What was that?"* The age of the atom, born within a bomb, had dawned.

Notes from a diary: "For more than two hundred miles the walls of the Grand Canyon are deep and precipitous. Some are sliced vertically, with sheer sides. Other peaks have jagged and forbidding crests. But the topmost levels are completely flat. They look like table tops high above the gorge bottoms thousands of feet below. The Grand Canyon is vivid with color. Most of all there is red and brown; but there are many surprising streaks of orange and even brilliant yellow, and along the canyon walls are unexpected areas of intense blue. In the wider and deeper canyons, enormous pillars have been carved by time and weather into many different designs and shapes. Other cliffs are neatly terraced in the form of giant steps. It is—especially from the air—a never to be forgotten sight."

A path to everywhere

A covered wagon in Wyoming country (*left*), just north of the Wind River—one man, one horse, and white-wall tires. The longest, straightest highway in America (*right*) runs across the flat Great Salt Desert of Utah.

Notes from a diary: "Westbound from Arizona's Gila Bend Mountains we flew over desert, through which winds the narrow Gila River. This area is known as the 'treacherous stretch.' For miles ridged, lifeless sand dunes reflected the afternoon sun with a painful glare. Years ago settlers built a wooden highway in order to cross these unmarked sands. Today the same area (*right*) still has remnants of the wooden road—plus a highway, canal, power lines, even a helicopter." Signs of the desert (*below*): trailer rigs on different paths in California.

Aerial ambassadors in blue . . .

Nowhere in America does nature present such sudden and unexpected contrasts as in the West. Along the border of Nevada and Utah are dark-surfaced mountains, of which Pilot Peak is the last barrier before an abrupt change takes place. The mountains come to an end, and in their place is white (*below*)—a long expanse of glaring light. These are the Bonneville Salt Flats of Utah.

Notes from a diary: "Millions of Americans have watched the Air Force jet precision team demonstrate the skill of the modern fighter pilot and his airplane. High over Nevada, a star-spangled blur rushes past our wing—an aerial greeting (*right*) from the Air Force Thunderbirds."

Fantasy in white . . .

Notes from a diary: "At the western edge of the Great Salt Desert, near the small towns of Wendover and Salduro, there is a turquoise expanse that reflects the glaring desert sun like a mirror. On this flattest of lands are the great Utah salt 'mines' that extend for miles as elaborately neat channels of water and chemicals (*above*). Swept by the sun the potash and other chemicals of the salt beds become iridescent glass sheets. Yet the real wonder of the Great Salt Desert is still to be seen. Across the Bonneville Salt

Flats the 'normal world' *vanishes.* There is no other word for it. A person's sense of balance and depth perception is lost as he gazes down onto the salt flats. These flats actually have a pattern, almost like mosaic white floor tile. Only, this floor is blinding white, with bare touches of off-shading. We drifted earthward into a sea of whiteness. Landing here was a strange experience. With the engine off and the door opened, there came the unusual sound of salt crunching beneath rolling tires. We walked

(*Right*) Lost in the vastness of Utah's Bonneville Salt Flats.

away from the airplane; the sensation was uncanny. All sound was gone. When we called to each other from a distance, it seemed that the whiteness swallowed up the sound of our voices. In the summer the Bonneville Salt Flats are baked as hard as stone. Each winter the surface becomes covered with water; as the water evaporates the remaining salt hardens to a fine, strong surface. These are the salt flats where the world's fastest cars race, where some men have streaked over the ground at more than four hundred miles per hour. For thirteen straight miles the cars roar along the salt bed; from the air a thin, faint line (*left*) identifies the racing course. At the south end of the salt flats is a long line of black telephone poles. Standing on the salt beds, looking in this direction, the viewer sees the most distant poles dropping lower and lower. The salt flats are so level that the decreasing height of those distant poles actually shows the curvature of the earth. During our visit, we sighted two trucks rushing toward us; one a Utah state vehicle, the other from a Texaco station in Wendover. They had watched our descent, assumed we were in trouble, and came on a rescue mission (*below*); *nice* people! When we took off, we circled the trucks (*left*); seconds later the whiteness absorbed them."

(*On following page*) America's loftiest mountains—the rugged, snow-covered Sierra Nevadas in California. ▷

A tiny train precariously hugs the side of this gorge (*left*) in the heart of the towering San Juan Mountains of Colorado. The locomotive is Engine No. 476 of the Denver and Rio Grande Railway. From Durango to Silverton the straight-line distance is forty miles; this original narrow-gauge train requires a full day for the round trip. (*Below*) In Montana's Little Big Horn country lies the hallowed ground of the Custer Battlefield National Monument. The cemetery at the top of the hill is the burial place of Custer and the band of men who died with him. Each grave marker on the slope is placed on the exact piece of land where a member of the Seventh Cavalry died.

Perched along the ridges of Mt. Hamilton, east of San Jose, California, is one of the nation's great astronomical centers—Lick Observatory. The body of its founder, James Lick, is buried beneath the foundation of the largest telescope. There are several white domes which house the telescopes of the Observatory, each assigned to a different research program.

Mountain to the stars

Farm fields during **harvest** (*above*), at Salinas, California.

Once barren desert (*below*), this is the Arizona landscape today.

Riches beyond compare

The greatest concentration of industry for the aviation and space age is found in the state of California. But the California soil still remains the bedrock of the state's economy. The agricultural industry still produces more annual income than does the production of jet airplanes as well as rockets meant to reach the moon, thanks to the rich, carefully tilled farmlands of the San Joaquin and Sacramento Valleys (*left:* citrus groves near San Bernardino). Even the California gold rush at its peak produced less wealth than their present-day orange orchards, though the largest crops of the state are cotton and vegetables. And to the farmers of the San Joaquin Valley, "white gold" is real—their vineyards produce ninety percent of our native wine.

Coveted coastline

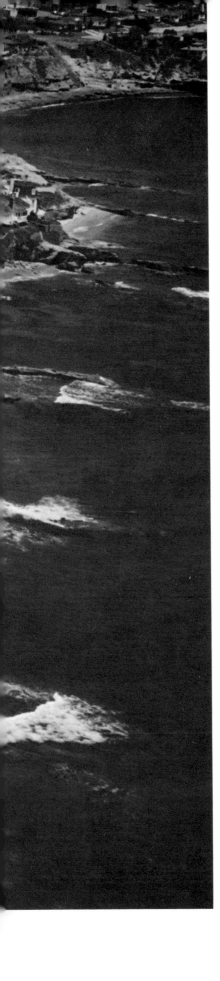

Homes along the rocky seacoast (*above*) at La Jolla, California. Traffic jam (*right*) in the sparkling harbor front of Balboa.

City of space and lights

Los Angeles, California, is rich in both Spanish and American history. It is also, say the engineers who plan tomorrow's cities, a look into the future. Its vast size (Los Angeles County is nearly four times larger than the state of Rhode Island) is an indication of the "megapolis" that will merge groups of cities into single communities. The late afternoon sun highlights the Los Angeles Freeway (*below*) in the city's downtown section. A new "pattern for living" shows (*right*) in a giant apartment project, one of several which now highlight the Los Angeles scene.

Dream homes on the

Los Angeles has long endured criticism as a city that has never known careful planning. The citizens of northern California, especially, insist that the Los Angeles area is more a hodge-podge than a well-designed community. Frank Lloyd Wright once remarked that: "If you tilt the country sideways, Los Angeles is the place where everything loose will fall." Perhaps in the past there was justification for this attitude, but it is no longer true today. There is now a "new" Los Angeles, in which a determined drive to utilize the talents of the nation's leading architects and engineers is paying handsome dividends. New buildings of modern design, beautiful landscaping, highway planning, community projects . . . all these are the signs of a city rapidly changing its character. Los Angeles reaches from the sea level of the Pacific to more than five thousand feet high, and its upper reaches are coveted for homesites. At the edge of Beverly Hills the mountaintops have been carved by bulldozers into sites for new homes. The building process makes the mountains look much like the temples of foreign lands.

production line

"Like a Japanese print . . ."

Notes from a diary: "Flying along the California coast, we turned at Balboa to begin a long ascent as the Los Angeles Valley appeared in the distance. The late afternoon sun transformed the haze lying in the valley and along the coastline into a strange mist. Sunbeams spilled to the ground in slanting golden shafts. Far to the west, off the coast, lay Santa Catalina Island. A low sea fog mixed with the haze to blur the shoreline of the island; from this mist a peak rose to more than two thousand feet . . . a scene remarkably like that of a Japanese print. The island's loftiest reaches seemed to be detached from the mist-shrouded land. At times this haze loses its aesthetic values for the people of Los Angeles, when it traps industrial smoke and fumes. But like most of the cities of America, Los Angeles has a major program under way to remove from its air the substances that can turn haze into smog."

The golden

hills

Many of America's coastal states have beautiful coast-lines, but California's is outstanding. Two examples are provided in the contrast between the Balboa Marina (*left*) and the Golden Foothills of the Diablo Range (*above*).

These hills lie slightly inland of the coast; to the west is the Santa Clara Valley, and San Jose. The hills are aptly described—in the late afternoon the sun turns their surface into one of burnished gold.

Fisherman's Wharf and Treasure Island

Of all the pier areas in California renowned for seafood, one of the best is Fisherman's Wharf in Monterey.

"The finest meeting of land and water in existence . . ." This was Robert Louis Stevenson's description of the coastline along Carmel Bay, the southern sweep of Monterey Peninsula. South of Carmel, the water around the cliffs is green and foaming white.

San Francisco America's favorite city . . .

Notes from a diary: "Like many of the really beautiful cities of the world, San Francisco is built upon coastal hills with a great harbor along its edge. The city stretches across more than twenty hills along a narrow peninsula. To the west is the blue border of the Pacific Ocean, on the east is San Francisco Bay, and at the city's northern edge is the channel of the Golden Gate. Often the mornings in San Francisco begin with a thick layer of clouds or sea fog hanging low over the city. But to the people who live here, the clouds are 'built-in air conditioning.' Before noon the sun often shoulders the clouds back to the coastline. (Looking toward the Golden Gate Bridge at exactly 11:00 A.M.: *right*) This . . . was a beautiful morning. The Golden Gate Bridge flashed back sunlight into the skies, and beneath the edges of the clouds three destroyers filed in from the Pacific, their greyhound speed cautiously reduced as they entered the harbor. A merchant freighter spread white foam as it moved toward some distant ocean port, and throughout the bay small pleasure craft winked bright sails."

186

City to everywhere: the Golden Gate Bridge (*left*) leads to Santa Rosa. Planes to the Orient and all points of the compass leave San Francisco International Airport (*above*). And waiting for heavier traffic flows (*below*) is this new complex superhighway traffic exchange.

Sausalito; looking south toward the Golden Gate.

Clouds roll in from the sea over San Francisco (*above right*), looking almost like a misty tidal wave. (*Right*) Alcatraz Prison in the harbor.

The mountain and
the reservoir

Lying in a deep, mountain-flanked trough, the Sacramento Valley
of California ends abruptly at its northern edge with Lake Shasta
(*right*). One moment there is rich farmland below—then, suddenly,
a curving wall of mountains fills the sky. Mt. Shasta, towering to
14,162 feet (*below*), can be seen over a hundred miles away.

The most beautiful mountain in

MOUNT ST. HELENS
—WASHINGTON

America

Timberland of the

Pacific Northwest . . .

The Pacific Northwest states of Oregon and Washington lead the entire United States in output of forestry products. In the midst of the timber tracts are surging rivers which provide power to run mills and yards (*right:* one of many dams of the Columbia River, borderline of Oregon and Washington). The extensive logging operations take place in the midst of the towering Cascade Range—beneath some of the highest mountains of America (*below:* Mt. Hood in Oregon).

For over one hundred years the timber crews cut their way freely through the stands of Douglas fir, Ponderosa pine, Sitka spruce, Western hemlock and the other trees of the Pacific Northwest. Large areas were denuded of their forest growth. Then, more than twenty years ago, a plan was begun to prevent the indiscriminate logging. This was the American Tree Farm Program whereby lumbermen use systematic methods to "tree farm" the timberland. Under the plan to preserve our forests, new trees replace all those cut down. But because of new scientific methods, the trees now grow taller and stronger, and we are creating new resources of wood faster than we take from the land. More than half of Washington's forests are still untouched. Oregon, richest in virgin timber, runs a lumber industry worth over a billion dollars annually.

Rainier . . . king of the mountains

Notes from a diary: "Dominating the Pacific Northwest is Mt. Rainier, known to the people who live here simply as 'The Mountain.' High over Seattle, Rainier appears to float on a bed of air. The effect of haze and low clouds, enhanced by the distance of many miles, obscures completely the low horizon; above the haze stands the white-domed peak. In the crisp air of early morning, we visited this impressive giant. All year round Mt. Rainier wears the ice sheets of seven different glaciers. When it catches the sun at precisely the right angle, an entire glacier reflects light as if it were a mirror standing thousands of feet high. In the summer the melting snow and ice become thin; silvery streams streak down from the upper slopes. Along the base of Rainier, the valleys and meadows are exceptionally beautiful. Large fields of wildflowers stand out colorfully against the background of forest green. The growth of trees and flowers ends abruptly at the mountain's higher, permanent zones of ice and snow. Here the ridges and crests are sharply defined, like waves that were frozen into place. As we flew away from Mt. Rainier— that great dome still visible more than a hundred miles away—the mountain seemed a sentinel guarding a corner of America."

. THIS IS MY LAND